One Race

One Race

There will only be one race of people in heaven, and that race is people.

Gerome Singleterry

Kravitz & Sons

INNOVATORS IN PUBLISHING, MARKETING AND ADVERTISING

Kravitz and Sons LLC
1301 Farmville Blvd, Suite 104
Greenville, NC 27834

Published by Kravitz and Sons LLC.

ISBN: 979-8-89639-156-2 (sc)
ISBN: 979-8-89639-155-5 (e)

Library of Congress Control Number: 2025906805

THANKS BE TO GOD

I would like to thank God for giving me the knowledge, the patience, and the wisdom to write this book. He deserves all the credit because I only write what he tells me to.

TABLE OF CONTENTS

PREFACE

There is a lot of tension in America and even other countries about Racism, God never intended for that to be. I wrote this book One Race, to show everyone here in America and the World that God has no preference of color or Race. When God sees us he only sees people, not a race. We are all created in the same image of God. I hope this book will help everyone to learn to love each other and never to look down on someone with a different color than yours and think you are better than them. Racism is planted in the hearts of people by Satan, not by God.

CHAPTER 1

NO RACIAL WARS IN HEAVEN

What is the true meaning of war? Webster's defines war as, "armed conflicts, as between nations, hostility or struggle, be in conflict" (Webster's Dictionary). There are so many wars being fought here in the USA and abroad. One of the most important is racial. God never intended for us to be at war with each other because of the color of our skin. In fact, he never even mentions color when he created Adam and Eve in the Garden of Eden. God was not concerned about the color of Adam and Eve's skin; he was only concerned about their hearts. He created Adam in his own image and then he created Eve from the rib of Adam. God did not say let us create Adam white and create Eve black. He never mentions what color they would be when he created them. There is no one that could tell you what race or color they would be before they were born. We are all created in God's image and anyone who hates another based on skin color has fault with God's creation. God never intended for people to be separated by race or color. I advise the people who do this to take their hatred up with the God and see what he says.

When God looks upon humans, he only sees humanity, not race or color because God created them equally. The last time I checked, all humans must eat, use the bathroom, go to sleep, etc. Now, how can anyone say we are different because of the color of our skin? Skin is only an outer barrier, not a defining characteristic of our being. However, where we do differ is in our hearts, souls, and beliefs. "So, God created man in his own image, in the image of God created him: male and female created he them" (Genesis 1:27) (KJV). Satan planted the seed of racism in the hearts of those people who would receive it—to bring a division between the people. He knew that if he could get people to become racially divided, they would become weak and he would win a lot of souls to hell due to racial hatred. Those who are racist are at war more with themselves and God than the people they hate because Satan has blinded them from the truth. How could any race think that they are superior to all other races when they did not even create themselves? The mere existence of a human being relied on the hand of God to create it. Those who think they're superior should look in the mirror. What makes them think they're superior to any other human being?

God did not create a race of people to be superior to anyone. There will be no racial wars in heaven and those who believe in racism will not be there. God loves everyone no matter what race they are, or what color their skin is, they are all the same to him. If you took a knife and cut an African American man, a Caucasian man, a Hispanic man, Asian man, or a Native man, their blood is the same color, there is no difference. This is what God intended for everyone when he created man in his own image, to view each other as equals. Satan has disrupted God's plans through the hearts of evil people, who allow him to use them. This is where racism begin—from Satan and the hearts of those people who follow him. Romans 2:11(KJV), "for there is no respect of persons with God."

Where do you think the idea of the Kul Klux Klan came from? Many people might say that it came from prejudice people. Rightly so, but man cannot think of anything on his own. There are only two spirits in this world that drives us—one is the Holy Spirit, and the other is Satan's demonic spirit. God would not give man a spirit of hatred and division among races because of the color of their skin, remember we are all created in his image. So that idea was planted by Satan. "But the fruit of the Spirit is love, joy, peace, longsuffering, gentleness, goodness, faith, Meekness, temperance: against there is no law" (Galatians 5:22-23) (KJV).

The idea of that one race is superior to all other races because of their skin comes from Satan. This organization was created by men who wanted to evoke terror into those who do not look like them. The idea of burning a cross in someone's yard in the name of racial hatred is tainting a sacred Christian symbol. This organization wanted to paint the appearance that God supported a racial cleansing of an inferior people. The people who engaged in this activity cannot truly be Christians or grasp the message of love the Gospel brings. "Thou shalt not avenge, nor bear any grudge against the children of thy people, but thou shalt love thy neighbor as thyself: I am the Lord (Leviticus 19:18) (KJV).

God would never bless anyone who does that; we are all human beings and should be treated with respect. Satan has his own way with those who do not know God. The Klan used a burning cross as a symbol in their organization which makes me wonder if they understand its significance? The answer is a glaring "no." Jesus was crucified on the cross, not to save one race, but to save all humanity. Anyone that believes that their race will be the only race in heaven, does not understand the heart of God. "Looking unto Jesus the author and finisher of our faith, who for the joy that was set before him endured the cross, despising the shame, and is set down at the right hand of the throne of God (Hebrews 12:2) (KJV).

When we were infants, none of us knew the color of our skin. We had to grow up and be taught that. Humans established racial descriptors. Look at the color black, there is no human being that black, look at the color white, there is no human being that white, now look at red, there in human being that red, and yellow, there is no human being that yellow. You see man created the color barrier the way he wanted to see it. This is where racism and separation began. God only wants us to be separated from sin, and not from each other. "Wherefore come out from among them, and touch not the unclean thing: and I will receive you" (II Corinthians 6:17) (KJV). The Jim Crow laws were created by evil men in the United States. God did not have anything to do with these laws, and he certainly did not bless the creators. Those who are continuing to think like that today will not be blessed. God created heaven, not man, so there will be no racial separation or racial wars there. God will never allow evil to come into his presence and disrupt his kingdom like Satan has used people to do here on Earth. There will only be peace and love for all people. Romans 12:9(KJV), "let love be without dissimulation, abhor that which is evil: cleave to that which is good."

"There is nothing good that will come out of someone that is racist; the only thing that will come from someone like that is evil. The Jim Crow laws were put in place to keep blacks and whites from interacting with each other. When the United States made this law, they must have believed God created people to be separated. This is so far from the truth, and only the followers of Satan would create such a lie and act on it. So those who continue to believe this, and are still following those laws, are followers of Satan. John 8:44 (KJV), "ye are of your father the devil, and the lust of your father ye will do. He was a murderer from the beginning, and abode not in the truth, because there is no truth in him. When he speaketh a lie, he speaketh of his own: for he is a liar, and the father of it.""

Adolf Hitler had the idea of the world being only one race. Now where do you think he got that idea from? You will never read in the Bible, where God said he only created one race of people for his pleasure. Satan is very crafty, and he knows how to go after people to get what he wants. Hitler was driven by the forces of Satan, so he really believed that what he was doing was right. Of all the races in the world, he went after the Jewish people first, which are God chosen people. "But ye are a chosen generation, a royal priesthood, a holy nation, a peculiar people; that ye should shew forth the praises of him who hath called you out of darkness into his marvelous light" (1st Peter 2:9) (KJV). Unless Hitler asked God for forgiveness for what he did to the Jewish people before he died, and how he felt about black people and people of color, his soul is resting in hell. He failed at what he was trying to accomplish with the extermination of the Jewish people, and those who believe in what Hitler stood for will also fail. Hitler forgot one thing; God was in control and not him. "No weapon that is formed against thee shall prosper: and every tongue that shall rise against thee in judgment thou shalt condemn. This is the heritage of the servants of the Lord, and their righteousness is of me, saith the Lord" (Isiah 54:17) (KJV).

Men start wars, not God, and those that are evil would want to start a racial war in heaven if they could. Just like Lucifer was cast out of heaven, God would cast those people out. But those people who have a heart like that will not make it into heaven. They will ultimately end up in hell, where they can start all the racial wars they want amongst themselves, and Satan will gladly be their General.

Revelation 12:7-9 (KJV), "And there was a war in heaven: Michael and his angels fought against the dragon; and the dragon fought and his angels. 8. And prevailed not; neither was their place found any more in heaven. 9. And the great dragon was cast out, that old serpent, called the devil, and Satan, which deceiveth the whole world: he was cast out into the earth, and his angels were cast out with him."

There will be no division in heaven amongst the people who make it there because their eyes have already been open to the truth. The world is still full of people that are prejudiced against people of color and who think they are better than them. God will never agree with anyone that has that kind of belief. He is the creator of all human beings. God loves everyone, but everyone does not love him. That is where the problem is. The love of God creates a wholeness in your spirit and a love for people of all backgrounds. He maketh the wars to cease unto the end of the earth: he breaketh the bow, and cutteth the spear in sunder: he burneth the Chariot in the fire" (Psalms 46:9) (KJV). God is love, and he did not create people to be against each other, or to hate each other. It is a shame that people throughout history have taught their children to hate people because of their color, mainly hating the African American people. Things have not changed that much in our society today, because there are some people still doing that. You would think by now they would have learned some sense and the truth about the Negro race. But there are some not willing to change their belief, no matter if it is true that they were taught a lie. "But speaking the truth in love, may grow up into him in all things, which is the head, even Christ" (Ephesians 4:15) (KJV).

Prejudice is an evil thing that Satan plants in the heart of people, which makes them hate other people of a different color with a passion. These feelings are often ungrounded, with no reasonable source. There will be a lot of people that will lose their soul and end up in hell because of being prejudice. This will not only be the Caucasian race, but any race that practices this. God has no favor in sin, so it does not matter what color you are. We are not just a token created by man; we are a living soul created by God that has a purpose. "Beloved, I wish above all things that thou mayest prosper and be in health, even as thou soul prospereth" (3 John 1:2) (KJV). Be careful how you view people and treat them. They did not create themselves and you are not their creator. God created them in his own image, and he was pleased in what he created. I feel sorry for those who judge what God has created. Just think about this for a moment, when you are doing that God is not pleased with you. "Be not forgetful to entertain strangers: for thereby some have entertained angels unawares" (Hebrews 13:2) (KJV).

An African American couple's children are just as good as a Caucasian couple's children. That is the way God sees them. There is no difference to him, and if you are seeing anything different, it is not coming from God. Satan has your heart, and your eyes are blinded from the truth and you do not want to see the truth. "Hell, and destruction are never full; so, the eyes of man are never satisfied" (Proverbs 27:20) (KJV). All the people that think they are better than all other people, please go and read your Bible. Your eyes need to be open to the true word of God, and then you will start to understand the truth. There is only one superior being in this world, and that is God. He created us for his pleasure and not for our own; we have no power to create anyone.

The people here in America need to stop judging each other, but come together and start loving each other. If this could happen, everyone would find peace and we would have a better country. None of us are worthy to judge anyone. We are all sinners saved by the grace of God. Only God is worthy to judge, but he forgives us more than judging us. People should stop thinking that their race is superior because of their color. It is not true, and it has never been. Satan will always be smiling when someone believes that. "But he turned, and said unto Peter, get thee behind me, Satan: thou art an offence unto me: for thou savourest not the things that be of God, but those that be of men" (Matthew 16:23) (KJV).

CHAPTER 2

A HUMAN BEING

Webster's defines human, "as being a man, woman or child", notice he didn't mention color or race in his definition. Caucasian men in the south referred to African American men as boys. Webster's defines "boy, as a young male -boy hood." In my opinion this means that a boy is not fully grown and does not have the maturity of a man, and he was treated like that. Webster's defines a man, "as a human being, adult male human." This tells me that a man would be someone respected as fully grown and in maturity and would be treated that way. So, what the Caucasian man was doing when he referred to an African American man as a boy, he was disrespecting him as a human being, and lowering him as a man. Romans 12:10 (KJV), "Be kindly affectioned one to another with brotherly love; in honor preferring one another." Animals are not human, but some people treat them as if they are and better than some people.

God did not create animals to be equal with humans. If he did, they would have been able to name themselves. God told Adam to give names to all the animals, because he was a human and had the intelligence to do so. Human beings are incredibly special to God because he created them for his pleasure, and in his image.

Genesis 2:19 (KJV), "and out of the ground the Lord formed every beast of the field and every fowl of the air; and brought them unto Adam to see what he would call them: and whatsoever Adam called every living creature that was the name thereof."

God created man in his own image, not animals. Genesis 2:7 (KJV), "And the Lord God formed man of the dust of the ground and breathed into his nostrils the breath of life: and man became a living soul." Now how can some people treat animals better than they treat some human beings? But this is what happened in this country to the Negro slaves. God was never pleased with this. That is why he allowed them to be freed. If God wanted humans to be treated like animals, he would have only created animals and not humans. There is no human being on this earth that deserves to be treated like that, black, red, yellow, or white. The human soul is a very precious thing to God, because he gave it to everyone, and it is a part of him.

2nd Peter 3:9 (KJV), "The Lord is not slack concerning his promises, as some men count slackness; but is long suffering to us-ward, not willing that any should perish, but that all should come to repentance."

People do not have a clue of what they are doing to a person when they gossip about them, even if it is the truth. James 3:6(KJV), "And the tongue is a fire, a world of iniquity: so is the tongue among our members, that it defileth the whole body, and setteth on fire the course of nature; and it set on fire of hell." Your soul is the most important thing you have. If you lose it, you will end up in hell. There is a judgment day coming for those who hate people because of their color, and think they are not worthy to be treated with respect. What makes someone believe that they deserve to be treated better than someone else because of their color? Those people are not serving the same God I serve; he will never accept people like that.

You cannot make God into something you want him to be and agree with your sins. Genesis 1:3(KJV), "And God saw everything that he had made, and behold, it was very good. And the evening and the morning were the sixth day." God created everything in this world, including all the people; he never said that the Caucasian race or any other race was better than all the other races. He intends for us to love, care, and help each other. This is what all people should do, no matter if you are saved or not. But people have their own way of thinking when they do not know God, so they are vulnerable to anything they hear. We were created to represent God, not Satan and the world. We should know better than that. Colossians 3:24 (KJV), "Knowing that of the Lord ye shall receive the reward of the inheritance: for ye serve the Lord Christ."

People who live their whole lives believing their race is better than all the other races and holding hatred in their heart for someone because of the color of their skin are led by the spirit of Satan. This type of behavior is not morally human. Think about a newborn baby. It has no control over what race it will be or what color it will be. But when the baby starts to grow up, will face prejudice from strangers the baby has never met before. I know this type of behavior is coming from the spirit of Satan, which these people have allowed to invade their hearts and their way of thinking.

Proverbs 23:7 (KJV), "For as he thinketh in his heart, so is he: Eat and drink, saith he to thee; but his heart is not with thee."

There are some Caucasian people still today that pretend they are not prejudiced, but deep down in their heart they are. They try to befriend blacks, but the truth of the matter is they still fill the same way about them. When they are around their white friends, they kind of shy away from their black friends and treat them different. What are they truly feeling in their hearts about them when they do this?

A true friend would never do that. We as human beings got a long way to go, and a lot to learn about how we should treat each other. Do not befriend blacks when your heart is not in it, because you are a liar just like Satan and would better off never befriending them.

Proverbs 18:24 (KJV), "A man that hath friends must shew himself friendly: and there is a friend that sticketh closer than a brother."

All my brothers and sisters are close, and we care dearly for each other. We, as God's children, are supposed to be brothers and sisters in the body of Christ. How can some Christians today have hatred in their hearts for some people they do not even know? Does that make any sense to you? But they are calling themselves Christians and must be thinking that God is approving of their hatred.

1st John 2:9 (KJV), "He that saith he is in the light, and hateth his brother, is in darkness even until now."

We are not worthy to be called children of God when we cannot even keep his greatest commandment. The Bible teaches us that God is love, and if we cannot show that to each other, we cannot be of God. God expects everyone that serves him to keep his commandments and walk in them. When you become a child of God, you are a mirror image of him.

John 13:34 (KJV), "A new commandment I give unto you, that you ye love one another: as I have loved you, that ye also love one another."

God already knows what is in our hearts better than we do, so you cannot hide a lie but for so long and then you will be exposed. Why hate when it is so easy to love? Ask yourself this question: Why do I hate people because of the color of their skin? Now, if you got a realistic answer that makes sense to you, keep on hating. But if you did not get a realistic answer that made sense to you, do not you think it is time to find God and get forgiveness for the hatred you have in your heart for no reason.

1st Samuel 16:7 (KJV), "But the Lord said unto Samuel, look not on his countenance, or one height of his stature: because I have refused him: for the Lord seeth not as man seeth: for man looketh on the outward appearance, but the Lord looketh on the heart."

I wonder how the white people would feel if the role was reversed today here in America. They would see how it feels to be mistreated by another race, just because of their color. You cannot tell someone you know how they feel when you have not experienced what they have gone through.

Therefore, everyone needs to think about how they are treating people, because one day it can happen to you. God delivered the children of Israel out of slavery and bondage from the Egyptians, and he did the same thing for the Negro race by delivering them out of the hands of the slave owners. Pharaoh and his army could not change what God had planned for the Israelites, and neither could the confederate states stop what God had planned for the Negro race.

Exodus 14:30 (KJV), "Thus, the Lord saved Israel that day out of the hand of the Egyptians; and Israel saw the Egyptians dead upon the seashore."

When God sees unrighteousness, he will move on behalf of those being subjective to it. God is not for unrighteousness, and he will not let it go unpunished. All people have feelings, and want to be treated with respect, even sinners. The Negro race has been mistreated by the white people trough out history, and they are still being mistreated today. I do not mean to single out one race, but history shows and tells the truth, and no one can deny that.

John 8:32 (KJV), "And ye shall know the truth, and the truth shall make you free."

Innocent human beings, who were beaten, tortured, disrespected, treated like animals, raped, and killed for only one reason: the color of their skin. Now think about that for a while and put yourself in their position. How would you feel? It would be hard to forgive anyone who has done that to another human being, but most of the Negro people have done it and tried to move on with their life and are still doing it today. But some of the Caucasian people here in America today want even to allow them a chance to do that. What does it take for people to understand that God loves all people, and you are better than no one?

Romans 13:10 (KV), "Love worketh no ill to his neighbor: therefore is the fulfilling of the law."

Those are people that will be judged by God if they do not repent of their sin and ask him for forgiveness. They need to understand, Negros are human, too, and God loves them the same way he loves them. Why repentance is so hard for some people when they know they are doing wrong, Satan really must have a hold on their hearts, and they are true followers of him.

Luke 13:3 (KJV), "I tell you, Nay: but, except ye repent, ye shall all likewise perish."

Anyone that is doing evil and not keeping the laws of God, and not willing to repent of that, will end up in hell.

CHAPTER 3

CHURCH RACISM

Webster defines "church" as a whole community of Christians. Church members, leaders and pastors that are divided because of the different races attending their Church are not of God. It does not matter what color or race you are, God created you, and in his eyes, no one should be treated with racism when it comes to attending church. What does color or race have to do with church services? Think about that for a moment. A church is a place of worship, not for hatred for other people of different color and race.

Romans 16:17 (KJV), "Now I beseech you, brethren, mark them which cause divisions and offences contrary to the doctrine which ye have learned; and avoid them."

Webster defines "racial" as concerning race or the difference between races—racism.

That is Webster's definition, not God's, because there is no difference in people with him. How can you claim to be people of God, and not want other people of color or different ethnic background to attend your church? The Church is a place for all those who desire to come and worship together; it does not have anything to do with what color or race a person is. It is a place to come and worship God and get salvation for your soul.

Romans 16:16 (KJV), "Salute one another with an holy kiss. The churches of Christ salute you."

I believe the pastors of those churches who agree with this racism in their church, should question there calling from God. God would never call anyone to preach his words that agree with this type of behavior, he would never bless any pastors, leaders or members who agreed with that behavior. Church is a holy place, and those who worship there should be aware where they are and who they are worshiping. God sees you when you are in church, and he knows what is on your heart when you are there. He searches the hearts of people every day.

Ephesians 1:18 (KJV), "The eyes of your understanding being enlightened; that ye may know what is the hope of his calling, and what the riches of the glory of his inheritance in the saints."

God intended for the church to be a place of worship for all people, with no preference for race or color. Those who attend church need to focus on what they are attending church for, and not bring segregation into the Lord's house. There is no place for this in the church, and certainly it will not be no place for that in heaven. Why would it be?

I know in my heart God is not pleased with those who practice this kind of behavior in their church. When we worship God, we are all human beings that worship him, so why would it be a problem for a black person or people of color to worship in a white church, or a white person to worship in a black church? We are all worshiping the same God; it does not make any sense to believe that people should only worship with their own race. It will not be like that in heaven, so what makes some people believe that is ok to do it here? But those people who choose to do that, so be it, but they need to learn not to hate or show racism to a person of color, or different ethnicity, that wants to attend their church. God has no problem with that, so why should they? When people do that, they are sinning, because one of God's greatest commandment is to love thy neighbor as thyself. God is not pleased with people who do this, and he never will be.

Ephesians 5:27 (KJV), "That he might present it to himself a glorious church, not having spot, or wrinkle, or any such thing; but that it should be holy and without blemish."

The churches that practice racism are not doing what God intended for them to do for his people. People who attend church are supposed to be Christians that represent God. Do you really believe you are Christian, when you do not want to worship God with black people, or any other ethnic race? Answer that question for yourself. That goes for anyone.

I do not think so, because a true born-again Christian would not act that way. They would show love, peace, and acceptance to anyone that wanted to worship with them and would welcome them with open arms. There are going to be a lot of people that think they are going to heaven but will be disappointed when they end up in hell, and a lot of those people are in the church. For instance, a racist who is not willing to change should stop trying to hide behind God and the Church. It will never work because God already knows how they feel and what they really believe

Hebrews 4:12 (KJV), "For the word of God is quick, and powerful, and sharper than any two-edged sword, piercing even to the dividing asunder of soul and spirit, and is a discerner of the thoughts and intents of the heart."

Those individuals might have come together as a group of people and started a church, but without God in it, it will never flourish. I do not believe God would want to be a part of a church that believes in racism. The church belongs to God, not man, and those who are not following his will, will not be blessed. People might think there are getting away with not allowing or wanting black people or people of color to attend their church, but God sees it all and he will be the final judge. There is nothing no one can hide from him; God knows and sees everything and searches your heart every day.

Matthew 16:16 (KJV), "And I say also unto thee, that thou art Peter, and upon this rock I will build my church; and the gates of hell will not prevail against it."

I am not trying to single out any race, but the truth is written in history. The church was created for all people who are willing to come together and worship God freely, without anger and hatred because of the color of someone's skin. Some people in America still have not understood this. God did not only create Caucasian people for his pleasure, but he also created all the people in the world for that. The government in acted the law of separation of church and state, but God never said separate the people of the church from each other.

Acts 2:47 (KJV), "Praising God and having favor with all the people. And the Lord added to the church daily such as should be saved."

The laws that man make are totally different from the laws of God, because they were created by people. Unfortunately, some people do not believe in God, and some of them are law makers. So, they create the law to benefit whomever they choose. You see, God would never make laws that only benefit one race of people. No, only men and women would do that led by the spirit of Satan. The people who truly know and serve God will separate themselves from sin and be blessed by him. God does not bless sin, and he never will.

1st John 3:9 (KJV), "Whosoever is born of God doth not commit sin; for his seed remaineth in him and he cannot sin, because he is born of God."

There are people in this world that confess to be a born-again Christian, but still hate people because of their color. How can anyone make a confession like that, and still have hate in their heart for people? I believe those individuals are lying to themselves, because deep down in their hearts, they know they are not really a born-again Christian. Racism is planted in their heart by Satan, and that is why people are not willing to change.

John 8:44(KJV) "Ye are of your father the devil, and the lusts of your father ye will do. He was a murderer from the beginning, and abode not in the truth, because there is no truth in him. When he speaketh a lie, he speaketh of his own: for he is a liar, and the father of it."

Is there anyone that can show me a reason that it would be wrong for black people to worship with white people in their church? The church is not the building; the church is in your heart and that is the people. God looks on the heart of man, not on the appearance of him because he knows appearance has nothing to do with what you are feeling in your heart and believe.

1st Samuel 16:7 (KJV), "But the Lord said unto Samuel, look not on his countenance, or on the height of his stature; because I have refused him: for the Lord seeth not as man seeth; for man looketh on the outward appearance, but the Lord looketh on the heart."

One of the things people cannot do is hide what they honestly believe and what they really feel, because God will make them reveal their true nature. You can only lie to yourself, because God already knows you are doing that, and it is just a matter of time before people will know that you are lying to. The things we really feel are deep within our hearts, and we tend to express some of them when we get angry. If you do not want to worship with other races in your church, you would be better off letting people know that, even though it is wrong. Just put a sign on your door, stating only white people can worship here.

Proverbs 23:7 (KJV), "For as he thinketh in his heart, so is he Eat and drink, saith he thee; but his heart is not with thee."

It is one thing to try to fool people, but to try and fool God is foolish, and that will never happen. You can read in the Bible where they tried to trick Jesus several times, but they failed. God knows what is in our hearts, and what we are thinking before we think it, remember he created us.

The woman that was caught in adultery was a sinner; and the Pharisees wanted to use her to see what Jesus would do. Most people today probably would have said, "She should have been stone to death." But Jesus was willing to forgive her. This is where the people, the Scribes and the Pharisees missed it. Jesus was always giving and willing to forgive anyone. They said by Moses' law she should be stone to death. But Jesus knew all her accusers had sin in their lives, so how could they judge her. So why do some people in their church try to judge people by the color of their skin.

John 8:4 (KJV), "They say unto him, Master, this woman was taken in adultery, in the very act." John 8:5(KJV), "Now Moses in the law commanded us, that such should be stoned: but what sayest thou?" John 8:7 (KJV), "So when they continued asking him, he lifted up himself, and said unto them, He that is without sin among you, let him cast a stone at her."

God wants all people to worship and praise him, no matter where you are, are who you are. He wants us to come together in unity and love each other, because that is what heaven will be like. If that means everyone worshiping in the same church building, by the grace of God, do it in the name of Jesus and Love. Never let a church building or some people divide your heart, because God never put a church building in your heart. He put the Holy Spirit there."

1st Corinthians 3:9 (KJV), "For we are laborers together with God ye are God's husbandry, ye are God's building."

My hope is that one day, everyone will be able to look at each other and only see another human being, and never see a difference in color again. What a wonderful day that will be, it might not happen in this world, but I know that is the way it will be in heaven. Try to remember this; the little children that attend church together both black and white, they do not see a difference in color when they are worshiping together. Why can't adults be like that?

Matthew 19:14 (KJV), "But Jesus said, suffer little children, and forbid them not, to come unto me: for of such is the Kingdom of heaven."

CHAPTER 4

SEGREGATION IN THE SCHOOLS

Webster defines "segregate" as "to keep apart from others."

Nobody should have the power to make a law, to separate people from each other in this world. But this is what the United States did when they created the Jim Crowe law. The law was created to separate the blacks from the whites, mainly from the Negros in the southern states. This is when segregation begins, because of a law that people created. God created all the people in his image, and only he has the true power to separate them. Who gave men and women this authority, not God, they were led by the spirit of Satan?

John 3:19-21 (KJV) "And this is the condemnation, that light is come into the world, and men loved darkness rather than light, because their deeds were evil. 20. For everyone that doeth evil hatter the light, neither cometh to the light, lest his deeds should be reproved. 21. But he that doeth the truth cometh to the light, that his deeds may be made manifest, that they are wrought in God."

The only separation God wants for his people is for them to separate themselves from Satan, sin, and the world. He never intended for people to be separated from each other, just because of the color of their skin. If he wanted that, he would have separated them himself.

Any God who would do something like that is not a God of love, but God is love, and his love is for all the people.

II Corinthians 6:17 (KJV), "Wherefore come ye out from among them, and be ye separate, saith the Lord, and touch not the unclean thing; and I will receive you."

Why would anyone want to bring segregation into the school systems, and teach young white children that it is not right to go to school with black children, or children of color? Those children are being taught something that will affect them the rest of their lives, and they are innocent. God will never agree with separating children from each other just because the color of their skin is different.

I feel sorry for the parents, grandparents, uncles, aunts, and anyone that have taught their children this kind of behavior. When children are growing up here in America, they should be allowed to choose how they feel about the situations that have happened here regarding racism. Not the way their parents, grandparents, uncles, cousins, and anyone else that wants to teach them to believe what they believe. That is wrong. It is the same thing as saying this what you must believe, right or wrong.

Proverbs 16:19 (KJV), "Better it is to be of a humble spirit with the lowly, than to divide the spoil with the proud."

The way some parents act and think, some children might see that as being wrong, and they would choose not to do that. If they want to go to hell because of their wrongdoing, that is ok, but they should try not to teach their children not to follow them there. When my brothers, my sisters, and I were growing up in Alabama, my parents never taught us to hate white people or anyone. Now I wonder how many white families in America can say they never taught their children to hate black people or people of color. When someone truly become a Christian, and they were raised that way, they would never teach anyone to hate another human being. So, are you truly a Christian, or a racist?

Matthew 5:44 (KJV) But I say unto you, love your enemies, bless them that curse you, do good to them that hate you, and pray for them which despitefully use you, and persecute you.

Notice in he did not say bless those who hate you, he only said do good to them. There is a big difference in the meaning of good and bless,

Webster defines good as being right proper, kind, beneficial. He also defines bless as "invoke divine favor for, approve heartily, confer happiness upon."

Do you really believe God would bless someone that tells a child, they cannot go to a school with white children because of their color? Hate is an awful thing, and God did not create it. The people who do hate crimes, and hate people without a cause today, are being led by Satan. A child is innocent and does not know right from wrong. It is up to the parents to teach them that.

Could you imagine what people would be like if they would have grown up not being taught racism? What a beautiful world and country we would have. Do not get me wrong, there are some white children that grew up in America that were not taught racism, it is just not enough of them were taught that. When you were a child, your mind was not on another child's skin color. You were too busy playing with each other, that had to be taught to you.

Webster defines "hate" as "dislike violently."

1st John 2:9 (KJV), "He that saith he is in the light, and hateth his brother, is in darkness even until now."

I grew up in a small town in Alabama called Jemison. We were not allowed to go to school with white children. I never thought about that as being bad or good, because I was happy being with other black children and going to school with them. When you do not know something is bad, it seems not to hurt you. But when you find out that it is bad, that is when it starts to hurt. One day I started to question myself, why couldn't we all go to the same school together, both blacks and whites?

Amos 3:3 (KJV), "Can two walk together, except they be agreed."

We as young children growing up could not understand why the white children were going to a different school. We also could not understand why we were going to a different school from them. It seemed like to us, we all should have been going to the same school together. See how innocent children are? I am quite sure some of the white children thought the same way we did, if they were taught right. Even if they were not taught right, I am sure some was thinking that.

You know, some children are wiser than what their parents want to give them credit for. Maybe if the country were run by children, it would be in better shape than it is today. Adults sometimes do have a way of messing up things that God intends for good. If the black children and the white children would have had their own way of doing segregation, we all would have all been going to the same school together. Do not teach your children something that you know is wrong. When you do that, you are only hurting them.

Matthew 18:20, "For where two or three are gathered together in my name, there am I in the midst of them."

The government started a program in 1969, which allowed the black high school students to choose if they would like to attend the white high schools. The first year I did not want to go, because I was afraid, so I stayed at my school. In 1970, I decided I was going to Jemison High School, because I did not have but two years left before I graduated. I wanted to play basketball before I left high school and attending Jemison High School was the only way I could play.

During the summer, I told my brother and my friend I was going to Jemison High School this year. My brother and my friend decided they were also going there. This made me feel more comfortable with the decision I made. Jemison High School is the white high school in my hometown and was not far from where I lived.

The main reason for me wanting to go there, I wanted to play basketball. My family did not have a car to get me to practice at Chilton County High School, where I was attending high school. This was an all-black high school, and it was about fifteen miles away in Clanton. This was the high school that black high school students that lived in Chilton County had to attend. We were bused there from our hometowns, in Jemison, Thorsby, Clanton, Maplesville, Verbena and Billingsly. It did not matter how far away you lived, you had to go there.

Joshua 24:15, "And if it seem evil unto you to serve the Lord, choose you this day whom ye will serve; whether the gods which your fathers served that that were on the other side of the flood, or the gods of the Amorites, in whose land ye dwell: but as for me and my house, we will serve the Lord."

When the students finished the eighth grade in Chilton County, it was then time for them to go to high school. The black students were bused to Chilton County High School in Clanton, Alabama. The same thing was done to other black high school students in their counties. The white schools in the south always had better facilities, because they receive the most money from the state and the counties. I wanted to go there to play basketball because I knew I would play. Black schools and colleges were always limited in what they could offer their students, because of the lack of funds they received. It was not fair back then, and it is still not fair today, but God has everything in control, and it is getting better.

1st Peter 5:7, "Casting all your care upon him; for he careth for you."

Where I lived was in walking distance of Jemison High School, and I knew I could get to basketball practice even without a car. I can remember my agriculture teacher telling us we would not have to worry about filling out a choice of school form for next year; because the government had made it mandatory that all the schools would be integrated. Why did it take so long for people to see the truth, and understand, that it would make sense that all children should be going to school together?

John 8:32, "And ye shall know the truth, and the truth shall make you free."

I believe the reason was, God wanted those people to see the truth about how wrong they were, and for the black families and the black students to be patient. Most white people probably thought that all black students wanted to go to their schools, but that is not true. Some black students did not want to go, and I was one of them. I was a good basketball player, and my talent was going to waste, because I could not play on the Chilton County High School basketball team. I could not get to the school to practice, because my dad did not have a car. I wanted to play basketball so bad, that I was willing to choose to go to Jemison High School that following year.

Romans 5:3 (KJV) And not only so, but we glory in tribulations also, knowing that tribulation worketh patience:

Romans 5:4 (KJV). "And patience, experience; and experience, hope:"

There should not be any segregation in schools or colleges in any country. Where do you read about segregation in the Bible? God did not plant that seed in the hearts of men. Satan did. There will come a day when men and women will pay with their soul if they do not repent of their sin and ask God for forgiveness for following Satan's lies about segregation.

There have been a lot of innocent children and families that have been hurt emotionally because of racism in this country. Not only black children and black families, but white children and white families have also been affected. There are some people who probably never agreed with segregation, and some whose hearts were changed. God bless all of them who did.

I Peter 3:15 (KJV), "But sanctify the Lord God in your hearts: and be ready always to give an answer to every man that asketh you a reason of the hope that is in you with meekness and fear."

When students are going to school or college, they are going there to get an education. They should not be worried about the color of another student's skin being different, because those students whose color that are different are there for the same reason. It is a shame what black students had to endure from white teachers, white students, and white families, when all the schools and colleges were forced to integrate. We were ok where we were, just did not have enough resources to have great schools and colleges.

The white should have understood. It was not the black families or the student's fault that they were forced to go to school with them. Although it was not wrong for the government to finally abolish segregation in schools and colleges in the south. Segregation in schools and colleges should have never been made a law. God would never have told men to make a law, to separate children from each other like that.

Proverbs 15:3 (KJV), "The eyes of the Lord are in every place, beholding the evil and the good."

It just goes to show you what people will do when they have so much hatred in their hearts. Some white people in the south really hated the black people and people of color. They hated them so much; they would not allow their children to go to school with the black children. What made them think their children were better than the black children, nothing but the spirit of Satan. So, in their own minds, their children were better because they were white? But not in the eyes of God, because he loves all the children. It is easy for Satan to use people for his service when they do not have the love of God living on the inside of them.

John 3:19 (KJV), "And this is the condemnation, that light is come into the World, and men loved darkness rather than the light, because their deeds were evil."

CHAPTER 5

RACISM TAUGHT

Webster defines "Teach" as "inform on a subject;" 2. "inform students regarding."

When babies are born, they do not have a clue what race they are or what color they will be and do not even care. But when they start to grow up their families will teach them what their heritages are. While they are growing up in their homes, whatever they see, hear, and are taught, is what they will start out believing. This is easy to understand where predigest and racism got their start in some people, but the seed was first planted in them by Satan. It was up to the people to change their way of thinking, if they desired to do so when they learned the truth, but many choose not to.

2nd Peter 3:18 (KJV) states," But grow in grace, and in the knowledge of our Lord and Savior Jesus Christ. To him be glory both now and forever. Amen."

To their credit, there were some white people that changed their mind about how they felt about the black people, and never believed in segregation or racism. God will truly bless those who did back then, and even today. Racism has changed a lot today, since I was a boy growing up in Alabama. But there are still some people even today that have not changed and will never change. This evilness is still practiced in the world and is still growing strong. I know that might sound crazy to some people, but it is true. When something is taught to someone, good or evil, it is hard to get it out of their heart.

Romans 12:21 (KJV), "Be not overcome of evil but over-come evil with good."

When white children grow up in a home, and all they here are how people of color, mainly black people, are no good, lazy, ignorant, a Niger, dangerous, bad etc., need I go on. Any child white, black, red, or yellow that grew up being subjective to that kind of teaching would soon start to believe it. Most black families would never teach their children to do that, but they would teach them the history of how their ancestors were oppressed and put into slavery by some white people, but not to hate the white people. When me and my sisters and brothers were growing up, my mom or dad never taught us to hate white people or anyone.

1st John 2:11 (KJV), "But he that hateth his brother is in darkness, and walketh in darkness, and knoweth not whiter he goeth, because that darkness hath blinded his eyes."

Why does color have such a powerful influence on some people, and will make them hate someone without any reason, other than the color of their skin is different from theirs. Just think about that for a moment and see, does that make any sense to you? The only reason I hate you is because the color of your skin is different from mine. Some people have been taught this from generation to generation. There is nothing wrong with the people's character, work ethic, honesty, and your faith. Just being hated because of your skin color is hard to bear, especially when you have not done anything to the people that hate you.

Hebrew 4:12 (KJV), "For the word of God is quick, and powerful, and sharper than any two-edged sword, piercing even to the dividing asunder of soul and spirit, and of the joints and marrow, and is a discerner of the thoughts and intents of the heart."

Racism is still here in America and some places abroad, because of one generation teaching the next generation how to be racist and hate people because of the color of their skin, because they were taught to do that. Some white families in America have done that, and some are still doing it today. Nothing has really changed in their hearts about being racist, and they are teaching their children to be the same way. Being a racist will never benefit anyone, but it will bring destruction to the people who are doing it one day.

Racism will be in this world until Jesus comes back for his church, and it will never be eradicated from the world, because you are dealing with a human heart. There will always be some people that will change, but not all of them. That is why some people will be in hell, and some people will be in heaven. When Jesus returns, those who are worthy will be caught up with him in the air, but those who are not worthy will be sent to the bottomless pit in hell with Satan. Will you allow something as meaningless as the color of someone's skin that is different from yours lead you there?

John 14:3 (KJV), "And if I go to prepare a place for you, I will come again, and receive you unto myself; that where I am, there ye may be also."

There are so many young black children here in America that do not really understand and know what racism really is, because they really have not experienced it in a degrading way. Like their mom and dad did during the 50s, the 60s, and the 70s, etc. How many black children in this country have been told to go to the back door to be served? Some of their families had to live it every day, and for some white families to continue to teach their children that today, is a tragedy. Why don't they teach their children about love and the truth, instead of hate and a lie? That is what God would want them to do, because he is love, and his love is for anyone who will accept it. The color of your skin has nothing to do with his love for you.

John 15:13, "Greater love hath no man than this, that a man lay down his life for his friends."

The people that are teaching racism, hatred, and violence to their children, beware. God is not blessing you for that and he never will. One day you will have to answer to him for those sins. This is not only for the white race; this is for all the races that do this. God is love, and he is not for racism, hate, or violence directed at any race. How can we teach our children to be Christians when we are teaching them to hate people because of the color of their skin? Are you serving the same God I serve? If you really believe you are a Christian, and God is blessing you and your family for this kind of behavior, Satan has you believing a lie. God would never do that.

1st John 2:4 (KJV), "He that saith, I know him, and keepeth not his commandments, is a liar, and the truth is not in him."

There are some good people in every race, and there are some bad people in every race, so I am not saying that all white peoples are teaching their children racism today, but what I am saying, the families that are not willing to change but continue to do this, are being led by the spirit of Satan and need to change. Those people should have realized by now, their ancestors were led by the spirit of Satan, and not by the spirit of God. Those who are led by the spirit of God would have never taught their children or grandchildren to hate people because of the color of their skin. They would only have taught them to love everyone.

Romans 8:14 (KJV), "For as many as are led by the Spirit of God, they are the sons of God."

Who I really feel sorry for are the people that are not like that being treated the same way as those who are, now that is unacceptable to me being a Christian? The racist people that have not changed their hearts about how they feel about black people and people of color should get what they deserve. But not the people who have changed their hearts and have asked God for forgiveness for what they have done. That was unrighteous to some people. Racism is taught, and it will always be taught by some people who have not allowed God to change their hearts.

Romans 10:3 (KJV), "For they being ignorant of God's righteousness, and going about to establish their own righteousness, have not submitted themselves unto the righteousness, have not submitted themselves unto the righteousness of God."

Do those scriptures sum up what happened here in America when it became a country? Everyone that is still racist, need to answer this question for themselves. Stop teaching your children and your grandchildren unrighteousness, because that is what you believe in and have been taught. When you continue to do this, you are bringing the judgment of God upon them for their future, and yours. The only laws that are still righteous and will never change were created by God, not by man.

When men create laws, they end up breaking them themselves. Just like when the government made treaties with the Native Americans they came back and broke some of those the treaties with them. They only did this when they wanted something back from them that was valuable, like the Black Hills of Dakota that had gold there. Some people are just evil and do not care who they hurt, as long it is not hurting them or their families. This does not come from God; he will never agree with those who do this.

Romans 10:4 (KJV), "For Christ is the end of the law for righteousness to everyone that believeth."

Do not be fooled by Satan. God is not like men who break their own laws. He would never do that, but he is watching those who do. No one that is evil and have done evil in the pass and have not asked God for forgiveness will never escape the judgment of God. Why would you want your children to be judged by God for their wickedness, hate and racism you have taught them?

Numbers 23:19 (KJV), "God is not a man, that he should lie, neither the son of man, that he should repent: hath he said, and shall he not do it? Or hath he spoken, and shall he not make it good."

How can a baby, around three to four years old, riding in a shopping cart with its mom at a grocery store say to their momma, "Look at that nigger?" Now you tell me if you really believe that baby was not taught to say that about black people. Now the baby is innocent, but the parents will have to answer to God one day for teaching the baby to say that.

Now when that baby grows up, it will have the chance to make its own decision about what is right or wrong regarding black people, and when the baby becomes an adult and chooses to continue to be racist, then the baby will have to face God for its own sins. Why would anyone want to teach a baby to hate any race of people? The people who do this need help in more ways than they can ever imagine.

1st Corinthians 13:11 (KJV), "When I was a child, I spake as a child, I understood as a child: but when I became a man, I put away childish things."

CHAPTER 6

RACIAL PROFILING

Webster defines profiling as "Succinct sketch of a person." Racial profiling does not only come from the police department, like most people might believe, it also comes from people of any color: white, black, red, or yellow. It said here in America that it does mostly come from the police department, and the white race. Why would anyone want to think that someone that is black is always up to something bad, or no good? How is that possible anywhere in the world?

Some white people do heinous crimes, for worse than black people. But if they are caught in a neighborhood not theirs, it's ok, and they are not treated as someone looking to doing anything bad or harm anyone. Think about that for a moment. Does it have something to do with what race they are and the color of their skin, that they can be trusted more?

Romans 2:11 (KJV), "For there is no respect of persons with God."

Now let us reverse that same situation with black people. It is not the same when they are seen in that same neighborhood; they are immediately suspected of someone looking to do something bad or harm someone. Now I ask the same question. Think about that for a moment. Does it have something to do with what race they are or the color of their skin, that you cannot trust them. Now you be the judge of that in your own heart.

Let me tell you what I think. I believe judgment has already been made about the black people, before the facts are clear for the reason for them being there. Clearly, this is racial profiling. Go take a survey of crimes committed by some white people and some black people here in America, and see what you find?

Has it ever occurred to some white people that those white strangers in their neighborhood could also be up to something bad or no good? That could be one of the reasons that some white people are vulnerable to crimes committed by their own race, because they trust them too much, they think they cannot do anything wrong. Color or race have nothing to do with the character of the heart of any human being, everyone is tempted with evil. So why do some people racial profile only people of color, and mostly the black race?

Psalms 118: 8 (KJV), "It is better to trust in the lord than to put confidence in man."

If people in America and the world would just slow down and ask God what to do before they act out their emotions, it would save a lot of hurt and pain to innocent people. I know there is some good in all people because God created them, but some people have allowed their goodness to be overshadowed with Satan's lies of evil. They refuse not to hear the truth, and most of them already know it, but they choose not to follow it. Satan's spirit is real, and he has got a hold on so many people and they do not even know it.

Romans 12:21 (KJV), "Be not overcome of evil, but overcome evil with good."

There is not a human being in this world worthy of judging anyone by the color of their skin or their race. God does not need anyone to that. He is the only true judge because he created man. Read Mathew 7:1-5 (KJV).

Mathew 7:1 (KJV), "Judge not, that ye be judged. 2. For with what judgment ye judge, ye shall be judged: and with what measure ye mete, it shall be measured to you again. 3. And why beholdest thou the mote that is in thy is in thy brother's eye, but considerest not the beam that is in thine own eye? 4. Or how wilt thou say to thy brother, Let me pull out the mote out of thine eye; and behold, a beam is in thine own eye. 5. Thou hypocrite, first cast out the beam out of thine own eye; and then shalt thou see clearly to cast out the mote out of thy brother's eye?"

No matter what the police departments say or the government officials, some white police officers in America racial profile black people and people of color, mainly black men. It is not rocket science to prove this; it happens every day in America. The officers that continue to do this is being led by the spirt of Satan and will face judgment from God one day.

Just to give you one example, my brother-in-law who has since passed, was driving in our hometown. He was obeying the speed limit; a white officer pulled out behind him and stopped him for speeding. While the officer was asking for his license, there were several cars passing by them at a high rate of speed. The drivers of those cars were white. The officer never paid any attention to any of them. Clearly, they were speeding. My brother-in-law told the officer that he needed to be stopping those people. The officer did not pay him any attention.

When some white police officers recognize black people in a car or a shopping mall, they pay special attention to them; as if they have already broken the law. You can see white people every day driving around you at a high rate of speed. Clearly, they are breaking the law but are not being stopped by the police officers. Black people and people of color are still being racially profiled by some white police officers in this country. The white drivers that were speeding never really got any attention from the officer, and they continued.

The white people need to think about that for a while and see how they would feel if that were happening to them. The racist white officers are too busy watching the black people, and people of color to do their jobs properly. What would be fair in a situation like this, answer that question for yourself?

Revelation 22:11-12 (KJV), "He that is unjust, let him be unjust still: and he which is filthy, let him be filthy still: and he that is righteous, let him be righteous still, and he that is holy, let him be holy still. 12. And, behold, I come quickly; and my reward is with me, to give every man according as his work shall be."

The white corrupt police officers that do this might think they will be able to continue racial profiling, brutality, and murder of innocent black people in this country, but they are going to be so disappointed when they are judged by God. He is already changing the government officials and the police departments. Notice I did not say man, because man's heart is not like God and will never change unless he is willing to allow God to change it. God has a plan for all the injustice that has been going on forever here in America. Get ready for a change. It is coming, and it is by God hands.

II Corinthians 3:18 (KJV), "But we all, with open face beholding as in a glass the glory of the Lord, are changed into the same image from glory to glory, even as by the spirit of the Lord."

You know, before the white people came to America; the Native American Indians were already here; some of the black and white people you see today are Native American Indian descent. The Native Americans and the blacks are not racial profiling white people in this country, so why do they have to be under this scrutiny? We were are all created equal by God, and we should be treated that way.

Webster describes scrutinize as "examine carefully—scrutiny."

The only people I know of that started racism here in America, is the white people, now I am not talking about foreign countries, they have some history of it, also. I am talking about America, where I was born and raised. There is no human being in this world that could not become racist, because it is a demonic spirit from Satan that is placed in your heart. All races have some people in them that are racist, but to single out one race of people or people of color, and torture them for only that, is wrong.

To hate people, murder people, racial profile people, give people a name nigger they do not deserve, you would have to be a follower of Satan's demonic evil spirits to do this. But in the end, all the people who do this without forgiveness will be judged by God in the end and there will be a price to pay. God will not allow any injustice to go unpunished by anyone, black or white.

Romans 1:2 (KJV) "Dearly beloved, avenge not yourselves, but rather give place unto wrath: for it is written, Vengeance is mine; I will repay, saith the Lord."

God is tired of this injustice in America, where the police officers can use their department to break the laws, some of the same laws they want everyone else to keep. I have no problem with police officers doing their job the right way and upholding the law for everyone. The problem occurs when they racially profile people of color more than their own race. This applies to all police officers, black or white. You know Jesus called the Pharisees Hypocrites because they were doing the same thing. What makes them better citizens when they are not upholding the law properly like they should?

Matthew 23:23 (KJV) "Woe unto you, scribes and Pharisees, hypocrites! For ye pay tithe of mint and anise and cumin, and have omitted the weightier matters of the law, judgment, mercy, and faith: these ought ye to have done, and not to leave the other undone."

When police officers or anyone that looks at the color of someone's skin, and judged them as being bad or no good, and looking to do harm without justifiable cause, is clearly racial profiling them. I know they need to find Jesus and the truth, but I believe they also need medical help. Why are blacks and people of color racially profiled? Can anyone answer that for me? Think about that for a moment. Why do some people think these races are the only race that is up to no good, all the time?

Some people have used different race and different color, as a means of hatred without any real cause for years. When will they realize that race or color has nothing to do with a person's heart, character, or soul? One of the biggest lies Satan has gotten some people to believe is that all people that are different from them are lazy, violent and no good. That is not true, that description is in all races. But some of the races bears the brunt of being treated like that. The negro race is one of the main races that has been targeted as being liked that.

Acts 26:18 (KJV), "To open their eyes, and turn them from darkness to light, and from the power of Satan unto God, that they may receive forgiveness of sins, and inheritance among them which are sanctified by faith that is in me."

We all know this to be true. There are some good people in all races and there are some bad people in all races, and it has nothing to do with the color of their skin or their race. Racist people choose to believe what they want to believe, no matter if it is a lie. But this does have something to do with the hearts of the people who are racist, and who are not willing to accept truth from God and change. God's desire is that all people should be saved, but some want, and will end up in hell because of their rebellious hearts and continue to follow Satan.

Isaiah 53:3 (KJV), "He is despised and rejected of men; a man of sorrows and acquainted with grief: and we hid as it were our faces from him; he was despised, and we esteemed him not."

"So, to all the people here in America and overseas that continue to racial profile people that are different from them, remember God will never be on your side and bless you for doing that. God is not racial, and how can some people say they love God, but have so much anger in their hearts toward other people that are different from them? I think they need to do a heart check when they say things like that, and when they are in church lifting their hands and giving praise and honor to God. People can spot a phony a mile away, but only God knows the heart and what is in it. We can never fool him."

Hebrews 4:12 (KJV), "For the word of God is quick, and powerful, and sharper than any two-edged sword, piercing even to the dividing asunder of soul and spirit, and of the joints and marrow, and is a discerner of the thoughts and intents of the heart."

Can anyone really think of justifiable reasons that would make their race superior over any other race? If we are ever going to live together in peace here on Earth, in love, and harmony, we must first learn to love God. All races matter to him, so repent of your sins, and give your heart to God and receive salvation. Then you will start to love everyone, no matter what race or color they are. Stop your racism and following Satan's lies. He is only leading you to eternal damnation in hell with him.

Luke 16:23 (KJV), "And in hell he lift up his eyes, being in torments, and seeth Abraham afar off, and Lazarus in his bosom."

There will be no racial profiling in heaven, so do not even think you are going there with that kind of heart. Believe me, there won't to be a place there for you.

CHAPTER 7

WHAT COLOR IS JESUS?

Webster defines color as "1. Property deriving from specific wavelengths of light. 2. Pigment. 3. Vividness."

As you can clearly see from Webster's definition of color, he never mentions a person or a human being. Color was given to people by man, not God. There is no human being in this world white as snow, there is no human being in this world black as tar, there is no human being in this world yellow as the sun, and there is no human being in this world red as a fire hydrant. Man created those colors for products, and God created the sun color. These are the colors man envisioned for the people God created.

They also did this with the American Indians, whom they saw as being red, and the Chinese people as being yellow. None of us could choose our skin color or ethnicity, but God could, and he did that for us. Have you ever noticed in the book of Genesis when he created Adam and Eve, he never gave them a color? The color of Adam and Eve was not important to him, because they were created his image and for his purpose. Color had nothing to do with their creations.

Genesis 1:27 (KJV), "So God created man in his own image, in the image of God created him; male and female created he them."

Now I cannot explain to you why God gave the people different skin colors, and different ethnicity backgrounds, but I can tell you he gave all the people a soul, and the same heart. When you read in the book of Revelation in the Bible, the description of what John gives of Jesus, it seems he was of a tan color, and his hair was white like wool. Since some white people judge everything by the color of people's skin and race, what color do you think they say Jesus is?

Read the following scriptures with an open heart and let the spirit of God guide you with understanding and truth. After reading it, what color skin do you believe Jesus had?

Revelation 1:10-18 (KJV) "I was in the Spirit on the Lord's day, and heard behind me a great voice, as of a trumpet, 12. And I turned to see the voice that spake with me. And being turned, I saw seven golden candlesticks; 13. And in the midst of the seven candlesticks one like unto the Son of man, clothed with a garment down to the foot, and girt about the paps with a golden girdle. 14. His head and his hairs were white like wool, as white as snow; and his eyes were as a flame of fire; 15. And his feet like unto fine brass, as if they burned in a furnace; and his voice as the sound of many waters. 18. I am he that liveth, and was dead; and behold, I am alive for evermore, amen; and have the keys of hell and of death."

Now to me, brass is not white like snow, black like tar, red like a fire hydrant, or yellow like the sun. To me brass is more like a brown or tan. Now brass is the color that John describes Jesus's feet, in those scriptures in Revelation. I know whatever color my feet are; my entire body will be the same color. John also describes Jesus's hair as being white like wool.

Webster defines brass as "alloy of copper and zinc."

Webster defines wool as "soft, curly hair, as from sheep's, goats."

Now if some people want to continue to believe their race is superior to all other races, they must be superior to Jesus to, because he is not white, black, red, or yellow. Try telling Jesus that your race is superior to him and any other race. What do you think his reaction would be to all the people that think that way?

Galatians 6:3 (KJV), "For if a man think himself to be something, when he is nothing, he deciveth himself."

When I was growing up, I used to wonder why every picture you saw of Jesus in our house or in the churches; he had white skin, with blue eyes, and long straight hair. Those pictures were painted and created by some men and women who wanted him to look like that. Those pictures do not even come close to what John describes Jesus as looking like in the book of Revelation.

That is not the true image of him, but the artists wanted people to believe that. Some people have always tried to hide the truth about the black race, and anything they have accomplished and should be credited to them. There is not anyone in this world that can say that Jesus looks like them, except maybe the Jewish people. The Bible teaches us that Mary and Joseph, Jesus' earthly parents, were Jewish. It is one thing we all need to understand: you cannot hide anything from God, good or bad. God is his own creation, no one creating him, man cannot create him to look like a man or a woman, because he created us in his likeness.

Psalm 139:12 (KJV), "Yeah, the darkness hideth not from thee; but the night shineth as the day: the darkness and the light are both alike to thee."

Jesus was a Jew by earthly ethnicity because his parents, Joseph and Mary, were Jews. Jewish people are not white, black, yellow, or red people. This is not about a race trying to claim that Jesus is their color, but it is about how some people think their race is superior to all other races. God did not create people that way, but Satan is using any race that will listen to his evil lies to believe that.

Acts 26:18 (KJV), "To open their eyes, and to turn them from darkness to light, and from the power of Satan unto God, that they may receive forgiveness of sins, and inheritance among them which are sanctified by faith that is in me."

During the time of Jesus's ministry while he was here on Earth, you never read in the Bible where he referred to people as being white, black, red, or yellow. Jesus was not any of those colors, and why does the color of someone's skin matter to some people anyway? We are all God's children created in his image, none no better than the other.

Being a white person, a black person, a red person, or a yellow person has nothing to do with your soul. God gave everyone a soul, and being any of those colors will not get you any favors with him. Notice how Jesus addressed the Samaritan woman at the well. He knew she was a Samaritan because they were in Samaria. He also knew Jews did not associate with Samaritans.

John 4:7 (KJV), "Therefore cometh a woman of Samaria to draw water: Jesus saith unto her, give me to drink."

Jesus never thought about how the Samaritan woman looked or what the color of her skin was. That was not important to him. He knew she was a Samaritan, and the Jewish people did not associate with them. This is a form of racism the Jewish people had against the Samaritan people. He also knew this woman needed to be set free from the sin she was living in. By him engaging in a conversation with her, he was showing his disciples and the Jewish people how to love everyone, including the Samaritans. Race and color have nothing to do with a human being that need help.

John 4:39 (KJV), "And many of the Sa-mari-tans of that city of that city believed on him for the saying of the woman, which testified, He told me all that ever I did."

The color of people's skin only matters to those people who are racist, and think they are better than all the other people who skin color is different from theirs. If this type of thinking continues in the hearts of people, there will be no place for them in heaven.

Because God knows all the sins, they have perpetrated against the people he created, and continue to do so even today. When Jesus returns for his children, believe me, he will not be shouting what color or what race you are. It does not matter to him what race you are, or what color your skin is, but what will matter to him, did you keep his commandments and do his will.

Webster defines perpetrate as "Commit be guilty of."

Acts 8:22 (KJV), "Repent therefore of this thy wickedness, and pray God, if perhaps the thought of thine heart may be forgiven thee."

You see, God knows that true repentance starts in your heart, and without it, you will never change. No, Jesus does not bear the color of the white race, the black race, the red race, or the yellow race, but he does bare the salvation of our soul. You will never read in the Bible, where it says that only one race of people will go to heaven because they are God's chosen people. But you can read in 1st Peter 2:9 what it says about the nation of Israel being his choice nation.

1st Peter 2:9 (KJV), "But ye are a chosen generation, a royal priesthood, an holy nation, a peculiar people: that ye should shew forth the praises of him who hath called you out of darkness into his marvelous light."

I know in this scripture, God was not talking about America; he was talking about the nation of Israel and the Jewish people. So why does color matter to some people, and make them hate people of different color so much? I believe it is not the people; it is the spirit of Satan that the people have allowed to enter their hearts with this hatred. If you choose to follow Satan, you will always be in darkness and full of lies and never accept the truth, and end up in hell with him.

John 8:44 (KJV), "Ye are of your father the devil, and the lust of your father ye will do. He was a murderer from the beginning, and abode not in the truth, because there is no truth in him. When he speaketh a lie, he speaketh of his own: for he is liar, and the father of it."

I am so glad that Jesus' skin color does not really reflect any people's color, because some would want to use that to promote their race as being superior to all other races. God created the people, not man or woman. Christian brothers and sisters and those who are not, let us start to show the world that the color of people's skin is not what makes their character, heart, and belief. It is what is in their heart, and what they believe and trust God for, that is pleasing to him.

Romans 10:10 (KJV), "For with the heart man believeth unto righteousness; and with the mouth confession is made unto salvation."

I believe we will never eradicate racism in America and the world, because we are dealing with the hearts of people. God gave everyone the power of choice, and it is up to the people to choose to do the right thing or not. If God had his way in every human being's heart and they accepted him, then yes, racism could be eradicated, but there will always be some people from all races that will reject him. That is why I do not believe it will never be eradicated until Jesus returns.

Isaiah 55:8-9 (KJV), "For my thoughts are not your thoughts, neither are your ways my ways, saith the Lord. For as the heavens are higher than the earth, so are my ways higher than your ways, and my thoughts than your thoughts."

Thank God he does not think like men or women, because those people that are still being oppressed by men's laws, because of the color of their skin would never get justice or be free. Any race of people in the world today that is facing this kind of treatment is just like the children of Israel when they were in bondage and slavery in Egypt. Psalm 103:6, "The Lord executeth righteousness and judgment for all that are oppressed."

For over two hundred years the children of Israel were at the mercy of pharaoh the king of Egypt, and his task master's whips. Pharaoh and the Egyptians thought that they would be slaves to them forever, but they were wrong. God heard their cry of agony, pain, and injustice from heaven, so he sent his servant Moses to deliver them. God does not approve of evil, and he will eventually deal with it, and the people who are doing it.

Exodus 3:7 (KJV), "And the Lord said, I have surely seen the affliction of my people which are in Egypt and have heard their cry by reason of their taskmasters; for I know their sorrows."

People need to be patient. God knows the sorrow, agony, pain, and the injustice that the negro race has suffered throughout history and is still suffering today. He is about to change the world now, for all the people that has been treated with injustice. Because there will be only one race of people in heaven, and that race will be the people who lived their life for God and made it there.

Exodus 3:8-9 (KJV), "And I am come down to deliver them out of the hand of the Egyptians, and to bring them up out of that land unto a good land and a large, unto a land flowing with milk and honey; unto the place of the Canaanites, and the Hittites, and the Amorites, and the Periz-zites, and the Hivites, and the Jebu u-sites.9. Now therefore, behold, the cry of the children of Israel is come unto me: and I have also seen the oppression wherewith the Egyptians oppress them."

Kidney, Walter C., and Laurence Urdang. Webster's New Compact Dictionary. T. Nelson, 1991.

EPILOGUE

I wanted to write a book that maybe could help ease the tension here in America about Racism that is very prevalent here in the South and also in other countries. One Sunday my pastor was speaking about the different races that attend our church. On my way home from church I got the idea to write the book, One Race. God didn't separate people by the color of their skin, that was men's ideas. If the hearts of people could only change and see others as being the same and not look at each other's color as a means of separation and being better than each other according to their race and color. If this could happen, could you imagine what type of world we would be living in. Racism would cease to exist and there would only be love for each other. (New Testament) 1st Peter 3:8 Finally, all of you, have unity of mind, sympathy, brotherly love, a tender heart, and a humble mind.

About the Author

Gerome Singleterry was born in Jemison Alabama, in 1953. His parents are Walter and Myrtle Sailes Singleterry, grand parents Ed and Ora Nix Singleterry, YC Sailes and Bertha Lowery Sailes. He graduated from Jemison High School in 1971, became a Christian at an early age at his Family Church Holly Grove Baptist in Jemison Alabama. He now attends King Wood Church in Alabaster Alabama, he is a born again Christian and truly loves God with all of his heart. He is Happily married to his wife Donna and they have three daughters, Gabriele a Nurse Practitioner, Stephanie Human Resources, and Tracy Fast Food Manager. They also have two grandchildren Destin, Computer Science, and Kayla a senior in High School. He has four brothers and five sisters, Walter, Andre, Steve, Douglas, Dorothy, Joann, Matha Ann, Kathy and Diann. He wanted to write a book that would show the world that God loves everyone and has no preference of color or race, and to help ease the tension of Racism everywhere.

www.ingramcontent.com/pod-product-compliance
Lightning Source LLC
Chambersburg PA
CBHW051240120626
46547CB00014B/1725